WUSHAN A PEARL OF THE THREE GORGES

三峡の明珠—巫山

三峡明珠——巫山

重庆出版社 ▲

目 录
Table of Contents

夔门秋色
Autumn at Kui Gate
夔門の秋

三峡明珠—巫山

对于来过三峡的朋友，这，无疑是一份最永恒的纪念品；

对于初恋三峡的朋友，这，无疑是一份最珍贵的见面礼。

因为，巫山高无极，三峡此为魁！

因为，神女虽无恙，高峡出平湖！

因为，旅游四十佳，华夏一奇葩！

……

巫山，地处长江三峡的腹心，是渝东与鄂西的天然界碑；

巫山，无论东进，还是西出，都是三峡观光的必经之地；

巫山，既是三峡揽胜的轴心，又是去小三峡和小小三峡的起点。

万峰磅礴一江通，

锁钥荆襄气势雄。

田野纵横千嶂里，

人烟错杂半山中。

巫山自然风光之美，集中体现在四个字：峰、水、云、石。

峰。上天之偏爱，巫山十二峰，几乎就是游三峡的代名词。"放舟下巫峡，心在十二峰。"这是古人的心声。"与其在悬崖上展览千年，不如在爱人肩头痛哭一晚。"这是今人的感叹。

水。水能载舟，更能醉人。前者为共性，后者则是巫山大宁河的特殊个性。大宁河水，养育美女，从古至今，名不虚传。就连祖国各地的打工妹队伍，只要沾上大宁河的灵气，就会与众不同。当然，王昭君沐浴在大宁河边的美妙传说，亦给游客心灵的渴盼染上几分神秘色彩。

云。巫山的云，奇妙无穷，春夏秋冬变幻莫测。无需堆砌形容词，朋友，请记住一句古诗：除却巫山不是云。

石。三峡石，便出自巫山。近年来，旅游部门推出的巫山旅游套餐：三峡读岸 — 徒步江边欣赏峡江两岸的奇石雕刻群，果真出奇制胜，游者惊叹：旅游三峡不读岸，等于白看两岸山！

如果说自然风光是上天对巫山恩宠，那么，民风民俗、历史文化，则是巫山的灵气所在。

— 巫山是世界人类的起源地。两百万年前的龙骨坡古人类化石，佐证了巫山系世界人类起源地之一的圣地；教科书引用的"大溪文化"遗址，更展示出巫山六千年前新石器文化的辉煌；还有县城随处可见的汉砖汉瓦，郊外的"三台"与"八景"，大宁河上的栈道，小三峡的悬棺，巫峡中的孔明碑，大昌古镇的温家院……都会让游人入梦心动！

— 巫山是巫文化的发源地！

— 巫山是巴文化和楚文化的杂交地！

— 巫山是三峡文化的根据地！

"行到巫山必有诗。"为我国伟大诗人、世界文化名人屈原的《九歌·山鬼》，便是歌颂巫山神女的最早诗篇。随后，又有楚国辞赋家宋玉流寓巫山时，留下了著名的《高唐赋》、《神女赋》。唐代诗人李白、杜甫、刘禹锡，都以自己的独特视觉与感悟，将巫山的自然风光勾画得栩栩如生，活灵活现……现代的一批又一批的作家、诗人、书家、画家纷至沓来，穿梭其间，虽有上乘之作见诸报端，但比起前人的千古绝唱，亦有自愧不如之虑。

三峡是一座金矿，旅者游者都能成为淘金者！

巫山是一部大书，旅者游者都能成为读书人！

以游为伴三峡行，以文会友巫山见。来吧，朋友，云雨巫山梦三峡！不信，有歌为证：

望三峡，你是那彩霞落九天

看巫山，我的天上人间

两岸猿声啼散了满江的云雾

惊回首，白浪排排洗蓝天

……

爱三峡，枫叶如火把水天红遍

恋巫山，我的天上人间

巫山神女千年不变的爱恋

感苍天，片片红叶寄思念

……

巫山云雨情切切

天外飞清泉

巫山，我的天上人间……

WUSHAN A PEARL OF THE THREE GORGES

It is no doubt the most durable souvenir for those friends who have been to the Three Gorges.

It is no doubt the most precious gift for those friends who love the Three Gorges at first sight.

Because: the Wushan Mountain is as high as the sky and the Three Gorges is on the top of it.

Because: if Goddess were still alive, she would witness a great and wonderful lake which will be soon completed in the Three Gorges.

Because Wushan is one of the 40 best resorts and a wonder in China.

......

Wushan, situated at the heart of the Changjiang Gorges, is the natural boundary tablet of the Western Hubei and the Eastern Chongqing.

Wushan, no matter you enter Chongqing westward or leave Chongqing eastward, is the only way for the travel of the Three Gorges.

Wushan, is at the centre of the Three Gorges tourism as well as the starting point of the travel to the Small Three Gorges and the Lesser Small Three Gorges.

A tremendous river passes through numerous peaks,
A magnificent mountain controls Jingzhou and Xiangyang like a lock.
Fields strecth thousands of miles,
the cooking smoke is from a farmer's house settled on the hill side.

The beauty of the natural scenery of the Wushan Mountain is concentrated into the four words, which are peaks, water clouds and stones.

Peaks : because of the love of God, the Twelve Peaks is the nickname of the travel of the Three Gorges. " Travelling down through the Wu Gorge by a sanpan, my heart is left at the Twelve Peaks". It is the ancient poem that expresses our ancestor's feeling. " I would rather like to weep against my lover's shoulder for one night than to be exhibited on the precipice for thousands of years." That is the people's sigh with feeling today.

Water: Water could charm people as well as support boats. The former is the general character and the latter is the special individual character of the Daning River of the Wushan Mountain. It is trully said in the past history that many beauties were brought up by the water of the Daning River. Even today girls from Wushan, who work in different places of China, look quite different. Of course the legendary story , which describes Wang Zhaojun, one of the four best beauties in the ancient China, bathing in the Daning River, leaves a mystery over the desire of tourists.

Clouds: The clouds over and in the Wu shan Mountain are unique, changeable and unpredictable all the year around. Friends, we don't want to use many adjectives, but sincerely hope that you could remember one line of the ancient poem as follows: " For clouds and fog, I have witnessed the Wushan Mountain."

Stones: The Three Gorges' pebbles, used as souvenirs, are mainly from Wushan. In recent years, the tourism department concerned in Wushan promote a new travel activity suit : reading the banks of the Gorges and enjoying the unique carving-stone groups while you walk on foot along the bank of the Changjiang River.

It is a real surprise for tourists: " It is a waste of time and money for those travelers who travel through the Three Gorges without reading the banks of the Gorges.

If the natural scenery is a gift from God, the folk custom and the historical culture are the soul of the Wushan Mountain.

——The Wushan Mountain is the birthplace of the mankind in the world. The Two-million-year-old ancient mankind fossils, found on the Dragon-Bone Slope in Wushan prove that Wushan is one of the holy places of the mankind birthplace in the world. The "Daxi Culture", quoted from the textbook, exhibits the magnificence of the 6000-year-old New Stone Age Culture. And the Han Dynasty bricks and tiles, easily found at the suburbs of the town, the suspending plank road along the Daning River, the hanging coffins in the Three Gorges, the Kongming stone Tablet in the Wu Gorge, the Wen Family House in the old town of Dachang etc., those above-mentioned things might carry tourists away.

——Wushan is the birthplace of the Wu Culture.

——Wushan is the crossing place inhabited by the Ba Culture and the Wu Culture.

——Wushan is the base of the Three Gorges' Culture.

"Traveling down to Wushan, a poem arises in my heart." *Jiu Ge, the Mountain Ghost*, composed by Qu Yuan, the great poet and famous literator in the world, is the earliest poem which praised the Goddess on the top of the Wushan Mountain. Later when Song Yu, the literator of the Chu Kingdom, composed *the Song of Gaotang* and *the Song of Goddess*. Li Bai, Du Fu, Liu Yuxi, many poets in the Tang Dynasty, from the different unique angles and with their own unique senses, described the vigorous and vivid natural landscape in the Wushan Mountain. Many calligraphers and painters traveled through the Three Gorges and composed poems and articles which were published in the newspapers. But compared with the famous long-lasting poems, the contemporary literatus feel that their own new poems could not match their ancestors' poems.

The Three Gorges is a gold mine where tourists could pan.

Wushan is a great book which tourists could read.

Traveling through the Three Gorges as a tourist and meeting friends as a fan of literature, friends, please come and enjoy the folk life of the Three Gorges which is proved by a song as follows:

I look at the Three Gorges which seems the colourful clouds from the sky;
and I watch the Wushan Mountain which is my paradise.
The screams of the monkeys on either bank scatter the mist and clouds over the river;
I look back and feel surprised,
the white waves are washing the blue sky.

I love the Three Gorges which is covered with red leaves;
and I love the Wushan Mountain which is my paradise.
The one-thousand-year lasting love of Goddess move God,
and red leaves are used as the substitute of missing.
......
The love stories in the Gorges are true and vivid,
Spring seems to fall from the sky.
Wushan is my paradise.

三峡の明珠－巫山

　三峡にいらっしゃったことがある友達に対してはこれが永遠の記念品である。

　三峡に始めていらっしゃる友達に対してはこれが珍しい贈り物である。

　と言うのは、巫山が高くて、三峡はここが一番である！

　と言うのは、神女は恙無く、高い山峡に平らかな湖が出る！

　と言うのは、よい観光地の四十か所の中の一つで、中華のめずらしい花である！

　………

　巫山：長江三峡の腹心地帯に位置され、渝東(重慶の束)と鄂西(湖北の西)の天然的な境目である。

　巫山：東と西へはみんな三峡の旅の経由地である。

　巫山：三峡の名所古跡の中心として、小三峡と小小三峡への出発点である。

　　　万峰は磅礴とし一江に通じ、
　　　荊襄に鎖鑰して気勢が雄し。
　　　田野を千嶂里に縦横し、
　　　人煙は半山に錯雑する。

　巫山の風景の美しさは峰、水、雲、石の四文字で現れている。

　峰：これは自然からの恵みである。巫山十二峰は三峡の旅の代名詞であり、"舟放ち巫峡を下れば心は十二峰にあり。"とこれは古人の心の声で、"絶壁で千年の展示よりむしろ愛人の肩先で一晩泣く。"とこれは現代人の感嘆である。

　水：水は舟を載せることが共性で、水は人を酔わることは巫山大寧河の特性である、ここの水は美女を育て上げることが昔から有名で、現在、全国に出かせげの娘たちの中に大寧河の霊気を染めると、普通の娘と違う。もちろん、王昭君は大寧河で沐浴した美しい伝説が旅人の心に神秘的な色を染める。

　雲：巫山の雲、巧妙奇抜、春夏秋冬に変幻極まりなく予測できない。友よ、古詩をおぼえ下さい、巫山のほかに雲がではない。

　石：三峡石は巫山の名物である。近年、観光部門から巫山のこういう観光コースを進めている、三峡読岸 － 川の岸で歩きながら両岸の奇石雕刻を楽めることである。三峡の両岸で歩けないと、両岸の山景色がはっきり見えない！と旅人が驚嘆している。

　自然風光は天からの恵みと言えば、風土民俗、歴史文化は巫山の魂である。巫山は世界人類の地源地で、両百万年前の竜骨坡古人類化石は巫山系の世界人類の起源地の一つを証明した、また教科書の上に使っている"大溪文化"の遺跡は六千年前の新石器文化の輝きを表わしている。町のどこでも見られる煉瓦と瓦、郊外の"三台"と"八景"、大寧河の古桟道、小三峡の懸棺、巫峡の孔明牌、大昌古鎮の温家院……旅人の夢と心を動ごく所である。

　－巫山は巫文化の発源地である！

　－巫山は巴文化(重慶)と楚文化(湖北)の混る所である！

　－巫山は三峡文化の根拠地である！

　"巫山にいたれば必ず詩あり。"とわが国偉いな詩人、世界名人－屈原の《九歌・山鬼》に巫山神女を歌う最初の詩であった。その後、楚の国の辞賦家の宋玉は巫山で住む時、有名な《高唐賦》、《神女賦》を殘された。唐の時代の詩人李白、杜甫、劉禹錫などはみんな自分独特の感覚で巫山の自然風光を生き生きと描かれている……現代のたくさんの作家、詩人、書道家、画家など巫山へ行ったり來たりして、優れた作品が新聞、雑誌などに載ったこともあるけれども、古人の絶唱より恥ずかしいと思う人がいる。

　三峡は一つの金鉱で、旅人はみんな淘金者である！

　巫山は一冊の本で、旅人はみんな読者になれる！

　旅を伴にして三峡へ行く、文化で巫山に友を会う、ようこそ、友達よ、巫山雲雨で三峡を梦にして、歌のとおりであろう。

　－ 三峡を望んで、あなたは朝焼けのように九天に落ちる
　－ 巫山を見て、わたしの天の世界
　－ 両岸の猿声は川の雲霧を散ち
　－ 観みると、白い波は青空を洗う
　…………
　－ 三峡を愛し、紅葉は火のように川を赤く染めて
　－ 巫山を恋し、わたしの天の世界
　－ 巫山神女は千年変わらぬ恋
　－ 天を感謝し、紅葉の葉は思いを寄り添
　…………
　－ 巫山雲雨は情あり
　－ 清泉は流れ飛ぶ
　－ 巫山、わたしの天の世界……

长江三峡
the Changjiang Gorges
長江三峡

中国只有一条长江。

长江只有一个三峡。

三峡系瞿塘峡、巫峡、西陵峡的总称。它西起重庆市奉节白帝城，东至湖北省宜昌南津关，绵延近200公里。

长江三峡雄伟壮丽、地形复杂、幽深险峭，各具特色。简而言之，瞿塘雄，巫峡秀，西陵险。

1500年前，郦道元所著《水经注》以最简洁的语言描述三峡的自然景观："两岸连山，略无阙处。重岩叠嶂，隐天蔽日，自非亭午夜分，不见曦月。"

In China there is one Changjiang River.

On the Changjiang River there is one Three Gorges.

The Three Gorges consists of Qutang Gorge, Wu Gorge and Xiling Gorge. It starts from the White King Town of Fengjie County of Chongqing Municipality to Nanjinguan of Yichang of Hubei Province, which covers the nearly 200-km distance.

The Changjiang Gorges is famous for its magnificent and beautiful scenery, complicated landform and deep valleys and precipices. In a word, Qutang Gorge is magnificent, Wu Gorge beautiful and Xiling Gorge dangerous. One thousand and five hundred years ago, Li Daoyuan, the writer of the Book *On the Geography*, with the tersest language, describes the natural landscape of the Three Gorges: " ... on either bank mountains are linked by other mountains with no cut. The range upon range of mountains hide the sky and the sun. If you stay in the Gorge, you could not see the sun and the moon until at noon and at midnight."

中国 に は ただ 一つ の 長江 が あり。

長江 に は ただ 一つ の 三峡 が ある。

三峡 は 瞿塘峡、巫峡、西陵峡 の 総称 であり、西 は 重慶市 の 奉節 の 白帝城 から 東 の 湖北宜昌 の 南津関、全長 200 キロメートル に 近い 距离 である。

長江三峡 は 雄大 で 壮観 である、地形 が 複雑、奥深く 峻険 で 独特 な 特長 が ある、要するに は 瞿塘峡 は 雄大、巫峡 は 幽深、西陵峡 は 険しい である。

1500 年前、北魏酈道元《水經注》の 中 に もっとも 簡単 な 言葉 で 三峡 の 自然 の 風光 を 表わした "両岸 に 山連なり、略闕る 処なし。重き 岩畳なる 嶂、天 を 隠し 日 を 蔽ぎる、停午夜分 に あらざる とりは 曦月 を 見ず。"

瞿塘峡
Qutang Gorge
瞿塘峡

夔门天下雄
the magnificent Kui Gate
夔門天下雄

风箱峡
the Bellow Gorge
風箱峡

瞿塘峡栈道
the plank road in Qutang Gorge
瞿塘峡の古栈道

重岩叠嶂
the range upon range of
mountains
重い岩、畳き嶂

夔门烟云
clouds and mist over Kui Gate
夔門の雲

轻舟已过万重山
A light boat has passed through
thousands of mountains.
軽舟己に過ぐ万重の山

巍巍三峡壁
the magnificent Three
Gorges' cliffs
巍巍な三峡壁

千姿百态的三峡石
the attractive Three Gorges' stones
いろいろな形の三峡石

巫峡
Wu Gorge
巫峡

巫峡烟云
clouds in Wu Gorge
巫峡の雲

巫峡信号台
a signal station in Wu Gorge
巫峡の信号台

巫山码头
Wushan Port
巫山の港

"曾经沧海难为水，除却巫山不是云"
" For water I have been to the blue sea, for cloud and mist I have witnessed the Wu shan Mountain "
曾て滄海は水が難しい、巫山を除く雲ではない

幽深秀丽的巫峡　▶
the deep and beautiful Wu Gorge
幽深で秀麗な巫峡

峡江晨辉
radiance at dawn in the Gorges
峡江の朝

峡江夜航
the night navigation in the Gorges
巫峡での夜航

春到巫峡
spring in Wu Gorge
春が来た巫峡

三峡之秋
autumn in the Three Gorges
三峡の秋

神女峰下
Goddess Peak
神女峰の麓

满山红叶映三峡
The mountains in the Three Gorges
are covered with red leaves.
山の紅葉が三峡を染める

千里江陵一日还
A hovercraft covers one-thousand-li
distance within one day.
千里の江陵一日にして還る

帰帆
A junk is returning.
帰って来た小船

峡江两岸美如画
the beautiful banks of the Gorges
巫峡の両岸が画のように美しい

峡江茶楼
a teahouse by the river in the Gorges
峡江の喫茶店

巫峡恋歌
the love song of
Wu Gorge
巫峡の恋歌

看三峡
enjoying the sights of
the Three Gorges
三峡を眺める

远眺神女峰
the distant view of
Goddess Peak
遠くから眺める神女峰

近观神女尊容
the close view of
Goddess Peak
近くから見る神女峰

孔明碑
Kongming Stone Tablet
孔明碑

箭穿洞
the Scissoring Cave
劍穿洞

集仙峰
Jixian Peak
集仙峰

巫峡群峰　▶
peaks in Wu Gorge
巫峡の峰峰

神女溪
Goddess Brook
神女溪

神女溪
Goddess Brook
神女溪

秋染净坛峰
Jingtan Peak in Autumn
秋の色は浄壇峰を染める

彩色的路
the colourful road
色取取な道

七里塘
Qili Pond
七里塘

神女溪观景台
the sight-enjoying stage
of the Goddess Brook
神女溪観閲台

神女溪风光
the landscape over
the Goddess Brook
神女溪の風光

西陵峡
Xiling Gorge
西陵峡

西陵峡
Xiling Gorge
西陵峡

雄关漫道(牛肝马肺峡)
the long and impregnable pass
(the Ox 's liver and Horse 's
lung Gorge)
牛肝馬肺峽

西陵晨曦
at dawn in Xiling Gorge
西陵峡の朝

黄牛峡之光
the light in the Ox Gorge
黄牛峡の波の光

水宽山远烟岚廻
the mist over the vast river and the distant mountains
水面が広く、山が遠くて雲が煙のようにまわしている。

晨捕
fishing at dawn
朝の魚釣り

葛州坝泄洪闸
the flood-discharge channel lock of the
Gezhou Dam
葛洲壩水利センターの洪水吐

葛洲坝船闸
the boat-channel lock of the Gezhou
Dam
葛洲壩水利センターのロックゲート

巫山历史
the History of Wushan
巫山の歴史

　　巫山是一座千年古城，历史文化积淀丰厚，自然景观比比皆是。
　　200万年前的古人类化石就发掘在这里的龙骨坡。6000年前的新石器文化遗址，就在这里的大溪镇；
　　大三峡中的巫峡，巫峡中的小三峡，小三峡中的小小三峡，如宝石，如珍珠，点缀其间，光彩夺目；
　　神女庙的威严，高唐观的神秘，大昌古镇的风情，无一不展示出巫山独有的品格和魅力！

　　Wushan is an ancient town with over a thousand-year history with the rich historical culture and many natural landscopes.
　　The two-million-year-old ancient mankind fossils were excavated in the Dragon Bone Slope here. The site of the 6000-year-old New Stone Age Culture is in the Daxi Town of Wushan.
　　In Wushan, Wu Gorge of the Three Gorges, the Small Three Gorges of Wu Gorge and the Lesser Small Three Gorges of the Small Three Gorges look as bright and shining as pearls and gems.
　　The dignity of Goddess Temple, the mystery of Gao Tang Temple and the folk life of the ancient town of Dachang exhibit the unique character and charm of Wushan.

　　巫山は千年の古城で、歴史文化の雰囲気は豊かで、名所古迹が多い所である。両百万年前の古人類の化石はここの竜骨坡で発現されたので、六千年前の新石器文化遺址はここの大溪鎮である。
　　大三峡の中の巫峡、巫峡の中の小三峡、小三峡の中の小小三峡、宝石パルーのように輝いて光っている。
　　神女庵の威厳、高塘観の神秘、大昌古鎮の風情、どこでも巫山独特の品格と魅力を現われている。

　　三峡工程建设加快，千年古城即将消失，成为美好的记忆。
With the quick construction of the Three Gorges Project,the old town,with the history of thousands of years, will soon disappear.
　　三峡水利センター工事の建設に従って、千年の古城は間もなく無くなり、これは美しい思い出として残こされる。

即将消失的巫峡镇（老县城)
Wu Gorge Town, the old county
town, will soon disappear.
間もなく水没する巫峡鎮

巫峡镇老城门
the old town gate of Wu
Gorge Town
巫峡鎮の城門

更替
the replacement
新い町と古い町の比べし

新县城一瞥
a glimpse of the new county town
見下す新しい県城

大昌古镇城门
the town gate of the
old town of Dachang
大昌古鎮の城門

古镇南门
the south gate of the
old town
古鎮の南門

古镇民居
the folk residence of
the old town
古鎮の住宅

巫山猿人遗址:
the site of the Wushan Ape-man
巫山猿人の遺址

大溪新石器文化遗址:
the New-Stone-Age cultural site
at Daxi of Wushan County
大溪新石器文化の遺址

威严的神女庙
the majestic Goddess Temple
威厳な神女廟

神秘的陆游洞
the mysterious Lu You Cave
神秘的な陸游洞

巫山出土的商代铜尊
the Shang-Dynasty bronze wine vessel, excavated in Wushan
巫山から出土した商代の銅尊

明代瓷器
the porcelain pieces in the Ming Dynasty
明代の磁器

汉代铜器
the copper pieces in the Han Dynasty
漢代の銅器

小三峡
the Small Three Gorges
小三峡

　　上天似乎特别偏爱巫山，不仅在这里雕塑出俊秀俏丽的巫山十二峰，而且在她身旁还精心雕琢出一个神奇缥缈的大宁河小三峡。

　　大宁河发源于大巴山南麓，幽深、秀美，宛如一位静谧的处子，养在深闺待人识，直到20世纪80年代，才徐徐揭开神秘的面纱。

God seems to love Wushan very much by setting up the beautiful Twelve Peaks in Wushan as well as carefully carving the mysterious Small Three Gorges on the Daning River.

The Daning River rises at the southern foot of the Great Ba Mountains. It is deep, quiet and beautiful like a calm unmarried girl who hides herself in the depth of the mountains and is unknown outside. The mysterious veil was not taken off until the 80's of the twentieth century.

　　天は特別に巫山を偏愛している、ここには美しくて、巫山十二峰かあるだけでなく、その側にもっとも神秘的な大寧河小山峡がある。

　　大寧河は大巴山の南に源を発し、幽深で綺麗、静かな処女のように世間の人人はまた知らないので、二十世紀80年代まで神秘的なベールを開らいていたのである。

小三峡秋色
autumn in the Small Three Gorges
小三峡の秋

龙门码头
the Dragon Gate Pier
竜門港

龙门峡
the Dragon Gate Gorge
竜門峡

天堑变通途
The bridge over two sides
of the Gorge makes the
traffic more convenient.
天然の濠を途と変わる

小三峡飞舟
a quickly-sailing boat in
the Small Three Gorges
小三峡の飛び流れる船

滴翠峡
the Vivid
Green Gorge
滴翠峡

宁河上游好风光
the beautiful landscape on
the upper reaches of the
Daning River
寧河上流の奇麗な景色

琵琶洲
the Pipa Sandbar
琵琶洲

秋染宁河
Autumn over the
Daning River
秋の色は寧河を染める

鸟瞰小三峡
a bird view of the
Small Three Gorges
小三峡を鳥瞰

竞渡
boats' race
舟の争い

深秋
autumn
秋

急水滩头百丈牵
trackers
船子たちは淺瀬との戦い

纤夫号子振峡谷
The songs of trackers echo in the Gorges.
船子たちの呼び聲

悬空倒看山峦影
The mountains are reflected in the river.
水面に山山の影が見られる

夏日
summer
夏

峡中小吃 "一条街"
a snack street in the Gorge
峡谷の中に軽食の町

画中游
traveling in the picture
画のような世界で遊ぶ

飞舟
a sailing boat
飛び流れる舟

过跳磴
crossing the shallows of the river
踏石を渡る

水帘洞
the Water Curtain Cave
水帘洞

玉帘飞花
The waterfall splashes down like a
jade curtain.
滝が落ちて、花のように奇麗い

小三峡灵动
animals in the Small Three Gorges
小三峡の可愛い動物

马归山
the Back-Horse Hill
馬帰山

青山绿水
the green water and mountains
青い山・緑の水

碧水轻舟
a boat on the blue
water
緑の川に軽舟

有朋自远方来
Visitors come from afar.
友あり遠方から来たり

拾到三峡石
picking up pebbles of the
Three Gorges
三峡石を拾う

飞云洞悬棺
the hanging coffins in the
Flying-Cloud Cave
飛雲洞の懸棺

宁河胜景美不胜收
the beautiful landscape on the Daning River
美しい景色が寧河のどこでもある

栈道·索桥
a plank road and a
suspending bridge across
the river
古栈道·吊桥

渡口
a ferry
渡し場

过渡
ferrying across the river
川を渡る

漁民炊烟
A fisherman is cooking.
漁夫たちの飲事の煙

放舟小三峡
A boat is sailing down in
the Small Three Gorges.
舟放ち小三峡

翠谷轻舟
a motorized sanpan in
the green Gorge
峽江の輕舟

宁河晚渡
ferrying   across   the
Daning River at dusk
寧河夕方の渡し場

宁河之春
spring over the Daning River
寧河の春

风景如画
the beautiful landscape
風景が画の如く

峡谷滴翠
the Vivid Green Gorge
緑の峡谷

大宁河流经巫山县城
注入长江
The Daning River
flows into the
Changjiang River
through the town of
Wushan County.
大寧河が巫山県を經由し
て長江に注ぐ

小小三峡
the lesser Small Three Gorges
小小三峡

马渡河发源于神农架北侧，自北而南流入大宁河滴翠峡，因明朝洪武年间农民起义军马分三路而渡得名。与小三峡一样，马渡河下段亦有三段景色各异的峡谷：长滩峡，秦王峡、三撑峡，于是，人们称之为小小三峡。

小小三峡风光原始，富于野趣，是现代人梦寐以求的世外桃源。

Madu River rises in the north side of Shennongjia and flows from the north southward into the Vivid Green Gorge on the Daning River. It gained its name because in the Hongwu years of the Ming Dynasty, the horses of the peasants uprising army were organised in three groups and crossed the river. Like the Small Three Gorges, on the lower reaches of the Madu River there are three parts of different gorgeous valleys which are named as Changtan Gorge, Qinwang Gorge and Sancheng Gorge so that people call that place the Lesser Small Three Gorges.

The wild and primitive landscape of the Lesser Small Three Gorges is a great attraction for tourists today.

馬渡河は神農架の北に源を発して、北から南に大寧河の滴翠峡に注いだのである、明朝の洪武年に農民いっきの軍隊は三つを分けて川を渡たることで名を付いたのである、小三峡と同じように馬渡河の下流に三つの景色違う峡谷があり、長灘峡、秦王峡と三撑峡で、人人はみな小小三峡と名づけたのである。

小小三峡は原始的な風光で、大自然にめぐまれて、現代の人人は梦にも求めている世外桃源である。

激流险滩
drifting down a rapid
漂流して速瀬を越える

世外桃园马渡河
Madu River, a paradise
世外桃源 の 馬渡河

齐心协力上了滩
Boatmen work as one to help
their boat up through the rapid.
頑張って淺瀬に登った

觅三峡石
looking for pebbles of
the Three Gorges
三峡石を捜す

乡土 "酒吧"
the country "bar"
郷土の "バー"

无处不飞花
a waterfall
どこでも滝が見られる

天生的人体艺术
the natural body art
自然的な人体藝術

长滩峡
the Changtan Gorge
長灘峽

激流勇进
A boat is driven against
the current
激流を乗り越える

巫山风情
the Folk Life of Wushan
巫山風情

神奇的三峡，迷人的巫山。

the mysterious Three Gorges, the charming Wushan

神奇な三峡、うっとりした巫山。

杀猪过年
preparing for the Spring Festival
豚を殺し、正月を迎える

农家院
a farmer's house
農家の庭

推磨子
grinding
石臼を引く

红桔丰收
the harvest of red tangerines
蜜柑の豊作

选种
selecting seeds
選種

编织
knitting
織物を織る

收工之后
after farming
野中仕事の後

背二哥
a farmer, carrying things on the back
山の中の交通は不便なので、山道の運送
はよく背負いかごを使り。

小卖
a vendor
売店

赶集归来
back from the market
市場から帰る途中

味道真不错
It tastes delicious
美味しいね

三峡农民喜迎亲
A farmer, a bridegroom in the Three Gorges, is happily carrying his bride home with a colourful sedan.
三峽農家の結婚式

小三峡艺术团
The Small Three Gorges Art Group
小三峽藝術團

编　　委：	王爱祖	侯长栩	黄　明	周世举
	石诗龙	刘大勇	彭顺清	侯小明
	谭开波	陈鸣放		

责任编辑：乔德炳

撰　　文：侯长栩

摄　　影：	乔德炳	方本良	孟学箴	包红明
	段荣昌	陆志富	晋守贤	高石汉
	解特利	宋开平	宋　军	李显荣
	李　健	李英发	高　松	徐光华
	吴恩周	骆　勇	张用庚	康光明
	乔森林	黎延奎	桂本运	李　晴
	王道中	吴　滨	冯　琳	李道友
	孙为和	朱智深	孔祥勇	谢　彦
	杨文龙	康文勇	周纯国	

英文翻译：张　辉

日文翻译：李　云

装帧设计：乔德炳

图书在版编目 (CIP) 数据

三峡明珠—巫山 ／ 乔德炳编 — 重庆：重庆出版社.2002.4

ISBN 7-5366-5737-4

Ⅰ.三...Ⅱ.乔...Ⅲ.巫山县—概况

Ⅳ.K927.194

中国版本图书馆CIP数据核字 (2002) 第020079号

三峡明珠—巫山

SANXIN MINGZHU WUSHAN

乔德炳 编

责任编辑　　周显军

重 庆 出 版 社 出 版、发 行

（重庆长江二路205号）

新 华 书 店 经 销

四川省印刷制版中心有限公司 印制

开本：787×1080　1/12　印张 9

2002年4月 第1版

2002年4月第1版第1次印刷

印数：1-3000册

ISBN 7-5366-5737-4／G·1862

0014000